MW00954502

A LITTLE GAVELS Guide to Agreements

# SHOULD WE SHAKE ON IT?

## Becki C. Lee

illustrated by: WALTER JACZKOWSKI

 scarlet oak press

scarletoakpress.com

scarlet oak press

ISBN: 978-954974-04-3 (e-book)

ISBN: 978-954974-06-7 (paperback)

ISBN: 978-954974-05-0 (hard cover)

Library of Congress Control Number: 2021916627

A Little Gavels Book (littlegavels.com)

Published by Scarlet Oak Press (scarletoakpress.com)

Listen now children
Pull your chairs near
Here's something to learn
Lend me your ears

Agreements and contracts
Help people to sort

Ideas and terms
They're long and they're short

Maybe your deal
Is with your older brother

Or maybe your neighbor
Can you help each other?

A contract has parts
That it can't live without

The first is an "offer"
Let's work it out:

If you help with my homework
I'll wash your mom's car

We both will be happy
It sounds good so far!

A's offer must be
Accepted by B
There's **no** contract until
Both parties agree

The goal is for both friends
To find common ground
If you don't "accept" you can
Just turn around

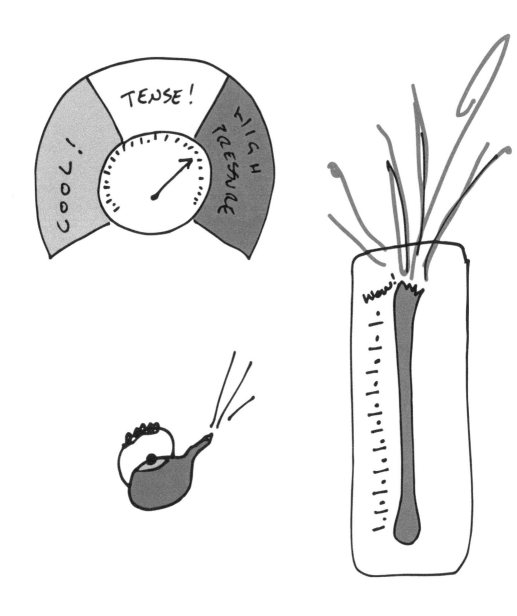

You **don't** have to enter
A contract unless
You want to and you are
Not under duress

Duress is like pressure
Or twisting your arm
You shouldn't agree if it
Will cause you harm

Here's a big word
You might love or might hate

Repeat after me, kid
Say "Nuh Go She Ate"*
(*negotiate!)

Your friend doesn't want
To wash that huge car

You offer your help
PLUS your spare candy bar!

Will that be enough
For your friend to agree
To help with your homework for
Basically free?

You could try **money**
Perhaps a dalmatian?
Lots of things can be the
"Consideration"

You probably should not
Be handing out pets

But you get the point:
You give and you get

That's consideration
Two things are exchanged

A promise is made
Payment is arranged

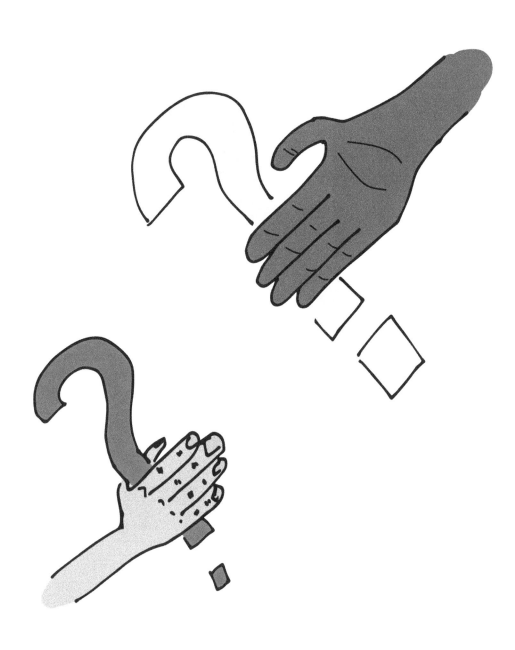

So, **should** we shake on it
My friend, think we should?

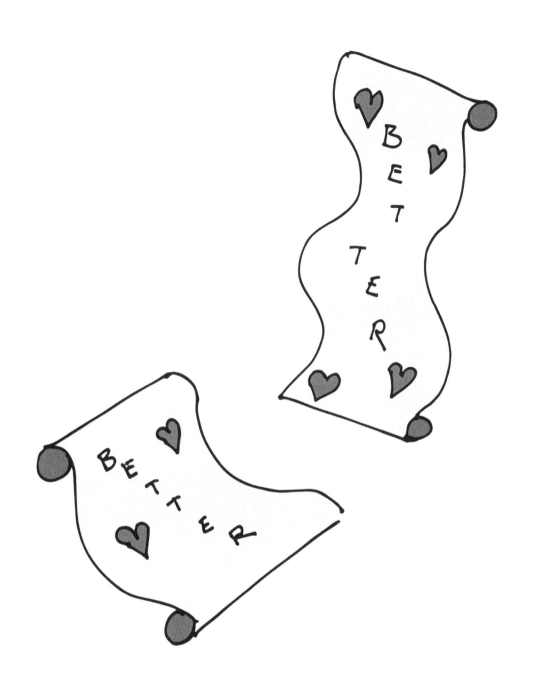

On paper is better
But handshakes are good

Don't sign your name
If you get a bad feeling

Your gut's your best friend
When wheeling and dealing

When you're an adult
You will be asked to sign

Or promise, agree, or
Meet with your minds

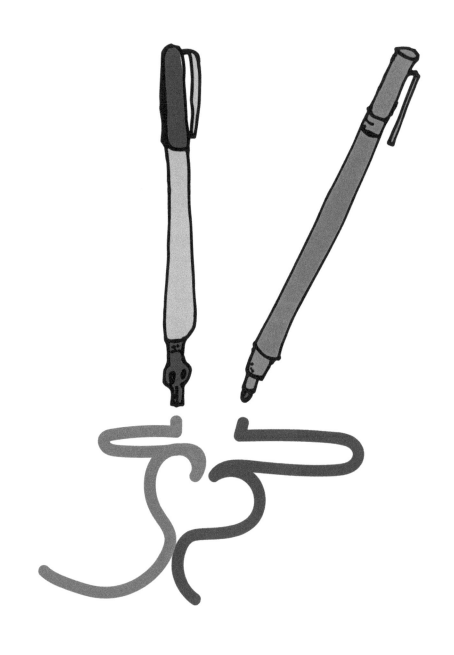

But please do your homework
(Yes, adults have that, too)
Before you write your name
In red or in blue

You will be happy
That you stopped to think
Before you signed your name
In permanent ink

These are the building blocks
That you will need

Now, go forth with confidence
You will succeed!

CPSIA information can be obtained
at www.ICGtcsting.com
Printed in the USA
BVHW020725191021
619200BV00017B/114

9 781954 974050